Dear L.

yo   'r

daily pick-me-up! you

are a precious friend. Love

to you always!

Lynne

June 15, 2021

Taylor Made

Thoughts, Truths, & Tidbits

365

Thoughts That Will Make Your Year!

Arden Taylor

Copyright © 2014 by Arden Taylor – Gray, TN
All rights reserved.

No part of this publication may be reproduced, stored in a
retrieval system, or transmitted in any form or by any means except for brief quotations in printed reviews without prior written
permission by the author.

ISBN 978-0-9906166-0-3
Design and Production
Riverstone Group, LLC, Canton, Georgia

Unless otherwise noted Scripture quotations are from the New
King James Version Bible.

Copyright © 1979, 1980, 1982 by Thomas Nelson, Inc.
Used by permission. All rights reserved

DEDICATION

This Taylor Made book, I dedicate to my Taylor Made family (one is missing in the picture). I acknowledge that God is the Creator, but I am grateful He allows us the privilege of procreation. As the gardener is responsible for the produce of his garden, parents are responsible for the character and conduct of their children.

I have no greater joy than to hear that my children walk in truth.   3 JOHN 1:4

CONTENTS

JANUARY

JANUARY 1

Daily devotion far exceeds yearly resolution.

JANUARY 2

The business of our EVERYDAY is to prepare for our LAST DAY!

JANUARY 3

Being baptized with the Holy Spirit means He is the RESIDENT of your life; being filled with the Holy Spirit means He is the PRESIDENT of your life.

JANUARY 4

Try Jesus, if you don't like Him the devil will take you back - (copied).

JANUARY 5

The only thing that is really worthy of my possession is that which I can have forever. The only thing worthy of my grasp is that which death cannot snatch from my hand.

Jesus said, *"Do not lay up for yourselves treasures on earth, where moth and rust destroy and where thieves break in and steal; but lay up for yourselves treasures in heaven, where neither moth nor rust destroys and where thieves do not break in and steal."* MATTHEW 6:19-20

JANUARY 6

Knowing the Bible is one thing,
knowing the Author is another.

JANUARY 7

If God is not the Creator there is no
hope for morality in this life. If Jesus is
not the Redeemer there is no hope for
eternity in the next life.

JANUARY 8

It's tragic when a person succeeds
before he is ready for it.

JANUARY 9

Joseph lost his job (GEN. 39:20) because God was more important than employment; because purity was more important than position; because holiness was more important than healthcare; because sanctification was more important than salary; because the Master was more important than money; because the Lord was more important than luxury; and because conviction was more important than cash.

JANUARY 10

In a marriage, lips should be used to kiss one's spouse, not to kick one's spouse.

JANUARY 11

Our purpose in life is not satisfied by the pleasing of man, but by the pleasing of God!

JANUARY 12

Faith is like a toothbrush; everyone should have their own and use it regularly. Using someone else's is dangerous and unsafe.

JANUARY 13

Our salvation is not built on a foundation of fantasy and feelings, but upon solid facts.

JANUARY 14

"God is revealed in the Bible as He is not revealed anywhere else. The person who has a closed Bible has a very limited understanding of God."
– Dr. Andrew Telford

JANUARY 15

The ultimate task of a preacher of God's Word isn't to fill the pews, or to fill a time slot on Sundays, but rather to fill up heaven!

JANUARY 16

Politicians want to be in step with the people; leaders want to be a step ahead of the people.

JANUARY 17

Fear is a poor chisel to carve out your tomorrows. Worry is simply the triumph of fear over faith. Worry gives a small thing a big shadow. Never respond out of fear, and never fear to respond. Action attacks fear; inaction builds fear.

JANUARY 18

"Some people go to church three times in their lives: when they're born, when they're married, and when they die – hatched, matched, and dispatched. The first time they throw water, the second time rice, and the third time dirt." – Adrian Rogers

JANUARY 19

God's provisions are a blessing, but even more than that they are a test; a test to see if we will increase our giving. God's provision does not mean that He wants us to find more ways to spend it, or more ways to indulge ourselves or spoil our children.

JANUARY 20

We are not to use the Bible as a hammer to pound others into submission to our rules and preferences, but rather as a light to guide others to the path of righteousness.

JANUARY 21

"The glory of the gospel is that when the church is absolutely different from the world, she invariably attracts it."
– Martyn Lloyd-Jones

JANUARY 22

Those who would say they are "pro-choice," deny choice to the very person who has the most to lose.

JANUARY 23

God is the greatest matchmaker. Just ask Adam and Eve.

JANUARY 24

"Every one says forgiveness is a lovely idea, until they have something to forgive." – C.S. Lewis

JANUARY 25

God delights in choosing the most unworthy and undeserving from among us to be the recipient of His unconditional love and grace.

JANUARY 26

God has an UNSELFISH LONGING to bless you because He has an UNCONDITIONAL LOVE for you!

JANUARY 27

A leader should be close enough to people to LOVE THEM, but far enough from people to LEAD THEM!

JANUARY 28

The operating system you have employed for your life is perfectly suited to produce the results that you are getting.

JANUARY 29

Because life is a puzzle Jesus says, "Come to Me and you will find the missing peace."

JANUARY 30

King David's sin was of such great rebellion and with such clever cunning, we would be astonished with him if we did not know the wickedness of our own heart!

JANUARY 31

It is no accident that Satan came calling when Jesus had gone forty days without food. *"He was hungry. And the devil said to Him"* (LK. 4:2-3). The adversary lurks in the shadows of our vulnerable moments.

FEBRUARY

FEBRUARY 1

If there is a Supreme Being who is higher and greater than humans, he has the right to determine what we are to believe and how we are to behave.

FEBRUARY 2

God will one day see to it that circumstances will champion character and condemn corruption.

FEBRUARY 3

When you study the words and messages of Jesus, it certainly appears that He was more interested in those He could count on rather than in those He could only count.

FEBRUARY 4

"The church is not a dormitory for sleepers, it is an institution for workers; it is not a rest camp, it is a front line trench." – Billy Sunday

FEBRUARY 5

"If sinners be damned, at least let them leap to Hell over our dead bodies. And if they perish, let them perish with our arms wrapped about their knees, imploring them to stay. If Hell must be filled, let it be filled in the teeth of our exertions, and let not one go unwarned and unprayed for."
– Charles H. Spurgeon

FEBRUARY 6

The Bible is a book about redemption. Had man not sinned there would be no need for the Bible for man would still be walking and talking with God as Adam did in the Garden.

FEBRUARY 7

And all the children of Israel complained against Moses (EX. 14:2). One of the burdens of leadership is to be unpopular when necessary.

◆ ◆ ◆

FEBRUARY 8

If you are afraid of criticism, you'll die with no accomplishment!

◆ ◆ ◆

FEBRUARY 9

"Your absence from church is a vote to close its doors." – R.G. Lee (paraphrased)

◆ ◆ ◆

FEBRUARY 10

God blesses us not to raise our STANDARD OF LIVING, but to raise our STANDARD OF GIVING!

FEBRUARY 11

"The Bible must have been written by God or good men or bad men or good angels or bad angels. But bad men and bad angels would not write it because it condemns bad men and bad angels. And good men and good angels would not deceive by lying about its authority and claiming that God wrote it. And so the Bible must have been written as it claims to have been written – by God who by His Holy Spirit inspired men to record His words using the human instrument to communicate His truth."
– John Wesley

FEBRUARY 12

"There are no 'small places' or 'small ministries,' and there are no 'big preachers.' But we do have a great God who can empower and bless servants who are dedicated to Him."
– Warren Wiersbe

◆ ◆ ◆

FEBRUARY 13

And now abide faith, hope, love these three: but the greatest of these is love (1 Corinthians 13:13). Why is love the greatest of these three? Today we need faith, but the day is coming for the believer that our faith will turn to sight. Today we need hope, but one day we will be in heaven and with the Lord, and on that day what more could we possibly hope for. Faith looks back at the cross. Hope looks forward to heaven. But love, it is for now, it is forever! Love is what God is!

FEBRUARY 14

Today most folks think about their SWEET HEART and that is good, but for me, today is my birthday. On this day in 1964 I got a SAVED HEART. It was on this day that by faith I accepted Jesus Christ and I was born again (John 3:3). My heart is tender and my eyes are wet as I think back to that night in my mother's bedroom.

Jesus' sorrow on the cross gave me joy.
Jesus' heart was broken so mine could be mended.
Jesus became sin so I could be clean.
The nails that held Him to the cross set me free.
The wounds He suffered brought me healing.
Jesus emptied His blood so He could fill my soul.
His crown of thorns made me royalty.

Jesus was rejected of men so that I could be accepted of God.

Jesus was stripped of His garments so that I could be clothed in righteousness.

In His fleshly body He gave me a glorified body.

He took on my life so that I could take on His life.

Hallelujah! Praise the Lamb of God who takes away the sin of Arden Taylor!

FEBRUARY 15

"I have decided to stick with love. Hate is too great a burden to bear."
– Martin Luther King, Jr.

FEBRUARY 16

Saints don't live for the here and now, but the there and then: not for this world, but for that world!

FEBRUARY 17

God may permit divorce because of unfaithfulness, but I don't think we could ever say, "God led me to divorce my spouse."

FEBRUARY 18

Forgiveness is not an emotion we feel, it is a choice we make.

FEBRUARY 19

God does not take a sinner to heaven because their works DESERVE it, but because His grace DECLARES it!

FEBRUARY 20

If God had wanted to consign Adam and Eve to Hell and start over, He could have. Instead, He chose to redeem what He started with – the heavens, earth and mankind – to bring them back to His original purpose. God is the ultimate salvage artist. He loves to restore things – and make them even better. His perfect plan is "to bring all things in Heaven and on earth together under one head, even Christ." – Randy Alcorn

FEBRUARY 21

"Being in power is like being a lady. If you have to tell people you are, you aren't." – Margaret Thatcher

FEBRUARY 22

Happiness is when you give others a piece of your heart...not a piece of your mind!

FEBRUARY 23

"Never allow the thought, 'I am no use where I am,' because you certainly can be of no use where you are not." – Oswald Chambers

FEBRUARY 24

The verdict in God's courtroom: He who pleads "not guilty" can hope to receive a fair judgment. He who pleads "guilty" can hope for a free pardon.

FEBRUARY 25

It's not the lustful look that causes the sin in the heart, but the sin in the heart that causes the lustful look.

FEBRUARY 26

The scripture says to be *"patient in tribulation"* (ROM. 12:12). It is always easier to know reasons why others should be patient.

FEBRUARY 27

Men want a faith that will change their circumstances; God wants a faith that will change us!

FEBRUARY 28

Purity is worth whatever price it costs to keep it.

MARCH

MARCH 1

"Give me a hundred men who fear nothing but sin and love nothing but God, and I will shake the gates of hell!" – John Wesley

MARCH 2

When we are RULED by sin, we shall be RUINED by sin.

MARCH 3

If the Bible is necessary to fallen man for the purpose of redemption, then inspiration is equally essential for our salvation. If our Bible is faulty, then so is our salvation!

MARCH 4

A big man is someone who makes you feel bigger!

MARCH 5

When your enemies throw mud at you, they are simultaneously losing ground.

MARCH 6

A world at its worst needs a church at its best!

MARCH 7

Responding to God's call will involve an altar on which some things we hold dear must be offered.

MARCH 8

The cost of following Christ is dying to self. The cost of not following Christ is to die eternally.

MARCH 9

The Golden Rule of marriage: What you want in your spouse, produce first in your own life.

MARCH 10

Forgiveness is actually pretty easy... until you actually have something and someone to forgive!

MARCH 11

Regarding a works salvation, everything depends on the SINNER; regarding salvation by grace, everything depends on the SAVIOR! Whom will you trust, yourself or Jesus?

MARCH 12

When God is your reason to live,
you will never have a reason to quit.
Copied

MARCH 13

Great leaders do not sit on top of
lesser men, but rather carry them on
their backs.

MARCH 14

Happiness means you have
something to do, something to love,
and something to hope for.

MARCH 15

If your purpose is not obvious, it is obvious that you have no purpose.

MARCH 16

"If God hadn't chosen me before the foundation of the world, He wouldn't choose me now!" – Charles Spurgeon

MARCH 17

If there's one thing better than getting an answer to prayer, it's being an answer to prayer.

MARCH 18

How are you to have faith in God
when you have so much faith in
yourself?

MARCH 19

Better to have a dirty reputation
and a spotless character, than to
have a clean reputation and a dirty
character.

MARCH 20

A good question for a Christians: if
real persecution comes will your faith
WIN OUT or WIMP OUT!

Consider Peter, just hours before he
denied the Lord he said to Him, *"Lord
I am ready to go with You, both to
prison and to death"* (LK. 22:33).

MARCH 21

"You might as well expect to raise the dead by whispering in their ears, as hope to save souls by preaching to them, if it were not for the agency of the Spirit." – Charles Spurgeon

MARCH 22

The life of Jesus was a road that began in a cradle, led to a cross, but ultimately to an empty tomb.

MARCH 23

Jesus had not servants, yet they called Him Master. He had no degree, yet they called Him Teacher. He had not medicines, yet they called Him Healer. He had no army, yet kings feared Him. He won no military battles, yet He conquered the world. He committed no crime, yet they crucified Him. He was buried in a tomb, yet He lives today. Author unknown

MARCH 24

Jesus transformed the cross from a symbol of FEAR to a symbol of FREEDOM!

MARCH 25

"Certainly this was a righteous Man," (Lk. 23:47). All the Roman centurion did was see Jesus suffer. He never heard him preach, he never saw Him heal someone, he never witnessed Him calming the wind or the sea, or feeding the five thousand. He only witnessed the way He died yet was convinced that Jesus was a righteous Man. A lot of folks can preach, but it takes a man of great faith and purpose to exhibit his righteousness while as he dies for others.

MARCH 26

God has placed the essential fact of Christianity on an unshakable foundation – the resurrection of Jesus Christ!

MARCH 27

Now when the sixth hour had come, there was darkness over the whole land until the ninth hour (MARK 15:33). In the daylight we see our Lord suffering at the HANDS OF MEN; in the darkness we see our Lord suffering at the HANDS OF GOD. In the daylight we see the INJUSTICE OF MEN; in the darkness we see the JUSTICE OF GOD. In the daylight we see man's hatred for the BEARER OF SIN; in the darkness we see God's hatred for the BURDEN OF SIN.

MARCH 28

Jesus is the way God got to us, and Jesus is the way we get to God!

MARCH 29

The death of Christ did not merely precede His resurrection; it was the price that obtained it. God *"brought up our Lord Jesus from the dead"* by *"the blood of the everlasting covenant,"* (HEB. 13:20). Jesus did not merely resurrect AFTER the shedding of blood, but BY the shedding of blood.

◆ ◆ ◆

MARCH 30

What did Jesus do on the cross? He satisfied the wrath of God; the curse of sin was fully absorbed; the price of forgiveness was totally paid; the righteousness of God was completely vindicated.

MARCH 31

"And if Christ is not risen, your faith is futile; you are still in your sins!" (1 COR. 15:17). The point of the resurrection proves that the death of Jesus is an all-sufficient price. If Jesus did not rise from the dead, then His death was a failure, God did not vindicate His sin-bearing work, and we are still in our sins.

APRIL

APRIL 1

The fool has said in his heart, "There is no God." PSALM 14:1

To be a fool does not mean to have little or no intellect, but rather to deny the revelation of God. To deny the evidence of the Bible as to the true nature of God, and substitute your own concepts for divine truth. The guilt of a fool is to harbor wrong thoughts about God in spite of the fact that He has revealed Himself to us.

APRIL 2

A Buddhist was converted to Christianity and asked why he changed his religion. He replied, "It's like this; if you were walking along and came to a fork in the road and two men were there and one was dead and the other alive, which man's directions would you follow?"

APRIL 3

Jesus hung out with a crowd of sinners and was hung up by the religious crowd.

APRIL 4

Legalism makes us proud of what we have done; grace makes us proud of what Jesus has done.

APRIL 5

In the flesh I'm really good at being bad. On the cross, Christ was really good at banishing that bad.

APRIL 6

Jesus' example teaches us that the greatest gift we have to offer is not clothes and jewelry, but rather the giving of ourselves.

APRIL 7

One thief was saved at death's door so none would dismay, but only one so none would delay.

APRIL 8

The cross represents the greatest possible TRAGEDY in man's dealings with God; the cross represents the greatest possible TRIUMPH in God's dealings with man.

APRIL 9

Jesus' work on the cross PROVIDED salvation for us; our work on the street is to PRESENT salvation to others!

APRIL 10

Just as Jesus' first coming was once futuristic but is now a historical fact, Jesus' second coming, which is now futuristic, will one day be a historical fact.

APRIL 11

All who misjudge Jesus will themselves be rightly judged by Him one day. Men continually misjudge Jesus, but He will never misjudge them.

APRIL 12

Throughout history man has tried to heal his sin-sick soul with the medicine of religion only to discover it's like trying to heal stage four cancer with an aspirin. Our hope is the Great Physician.

APRIL 13

"Between here and heaven, every minute that the Christian lives will be a minute of grace." – Charles Spurgeon

APRIL 14

Isn't it interesting that Easter usually falls in close proximity to the deadline for our income tax return? What a contrast. God is the greatest giver, government the greatest taker.

APRIL 15

A government that is big enough to give you everything you think you need, is also big enough to take everything you have.

APRIL 16

If the blood of Jesus does not cleanse the sin of others, then it cannot cleanse my sin either.

APRIL 17

We cannot help being "in Adam."
This is the result of our first birth over
which we had no choice. But we can
choose not to remain "in Adam." This
is the result of the second birth that
makes us "in Christ."

APRIL 18

In the FIRST world, man was sinless until
tested, and then became sinful and
imperfect leading to death. In the
FINAL world, man who was once sinful
and experiences salvation and is now
made perfect and equipped to live
eternally.

APRIL 19

Believers are overwhelmed by the PROMINENCE of the cross; unbelievers should be overwhelmed by the PEOPLE of the cross.

APRIL 20

From the cross Jesus said, *"Father, forgive them, for they do not know what they do"* (LK. 23:34). Many a man has cried out to God for forgiveness upon death, but not Jesus. He cried out for our forgiveness, but not for His own, for He was sinless. Here we see that we are responsible for our sin even if we are ignorant of our sin. You may be ignorant of Christ, of salvation, of the Bible, and of heaven and hell, but ignorance is not innocence. You and I stand in great need of God's forgiveness!

APRIL 21

As Jesus hung on the cross between two thieves, He said to one thief, *"Assuredly, I say to you, today you will be with Me in Paradise"* (LK. 23:43). Here was man who was an outcast, a felon, a man with a tainted past, a tarnished name, and a cursing mouth. Yet he will walk with Jesus in Paradise. This thief who spent his last evening on earth in the gloom of a dungeon, will spend his next morning in the glory of Paradise, from the darkness of a jail to the light of Jesus. It is no wonder the apostle Paul wrote, *where sin abounded, grace abounded much more* (ROM. 5:20).

APRIL 22

While hanging on the cross, Jesus seeing His mother said, *"Woman, behold your son!"* and then seeing His disciple Jesus said, *"Behold your mother!"* (LK. 23:34). While hanging on the cross to meet the eternal need of all mankind, Jesus would not forget the temporal need of His mother.

Interestingly, Jesus never called Mary "mother." He called her "woman." Jesus' greatest benefit to Mary was not in His role as her SON, but as her SAVIOR. Mary would later have more sons, but she could never have another savior.

APRIL 23

At the end of three hours of a mysterious darkness that covered the earth, Jesus cried out with a loud voice saying, *"Eloi, Eloi, lama sabachthani?" which is translated, 'My God, My God, why have You forsaken Me?'"* (MK. 15:34). Early in Jesus' earthly ministry we hear God the Father say, *"This is My beloved Son, in whom I am well pleased"* (MATT. 3:17). But now God the Father had to forsake His only begotten Son because there on that cross Jesus bore my sin and the sin of the world. In that moment, God the Father who could not look upon the sin that Jesus had become, and forsook Him. In that moment, Jesus became an orphan so that you and I could become the adopted children of God.

APRIL 24

After this, Jesus, knowing that all things were now accomplished, that the Scripture might be fulfilled, said, "I thirst" (JN. 19:28). That Jesus knew *all things* reveals His deity. He was the Son of God. He was Immanuel, God with us. That Jesus was thirsty reveals His humanity. He was the Son of Man. Imagine the Creator of the universe needing a drink of water.

Jesus began His earthly ministry by hungering (MATT. 4:2), and ended His earthly ministry by thirsting.

APRIL 25

The very first words that Scripture records that Jesus spoke occurred when He was twelve years old. Jesus said to His parents, *"Did you not know that I must be about My Father's business?"* (LK. 2:49). Now on the cross, and at the approximate age of thirty-three, Jesus spoke His last words before His death, *"It is finished!" And bowing His head, He gave up His spirit* (JN.19:30). With His shed blood and death, Jesus now had finished the Father's business...the business of saving us from our sin. Hallelujah! What a Savior!

APRIL 26

The revelation of God's Word has
already taken place – that's past
tense. The inspiration of God's Word's
has already taken place – that's past
tense. The illumination of God's Word
is still taking place everyday – that's
present tense.

APRIL 27

Failure is the result of thinking without
doing, or doing without thinking.

APRIL 28

When your head sticks above the
crowd, expect more criticism than
bouquets. Satan always attacks those
who can hurt him the most.

APRIL 29

The church is made up of sinners....
who finally admit it.

APRIL 30

It is impossible for a pastor to preach
biblical sermons that he doesn't
desperately need himself.

MAY

MAY 1

A man can go to hell UNSAVED, but he can never go to hell UNLOVED! *"For God so loved the world that He gave His only begotten Son..."* (JN. 3:16).

MAY 2

In the case of adultery, divorce was a concession for the innocent party, not a command to the innocent party.

MAY 3

It is impossible to forgive someone when you think of yourself superior to him or her, and that you would never do anything as bad as they have done. The older brother of the prodigal son is proof of this (LUKE 15).

MAY 4

When you think you merit God's favor, you will begrudge God's grace being given to others (MATT. 20:12).

MAY 5

God goes to great lengths to develop character in those He would assign to high places.

MAY 6

It is a blessing to possess a noble vision. But unless you manage yourself and the vision along the journey, it can turn on you and devour you.

MAY 7

Our greatest goal is to become, not to acquire. Jesus never taught us how to make a living, He taught us how to live.

MAY 8

Teaching a child to stand on his own two feet does not obligate parents to supply the shoes forever.

MAY 9

The problem with most children is that they grow up but they have never been raised.

MAY 10

The Christian home is to be structured by the dictates of scripture, not by the dictates of society.

MAY 11

Children who defy and disobey their parents will go on to defy and disobey other authorities.

MAY 12

One woman approached a mother with her young son and said, "My, your child is well-behaved, and he's loaded with self-esteem! Do you applaud him often?" The mother replied, "Yes, with one hand!"

MAY 13

A switch controls everything in our homes...except the kids!

MAY 14

"I remember my mother's prayers and they have always followed me. They have clung to me all my life."
– Abraham Lincoln

MAY 15

Jesus told us WHAT to do, *"you shall be witnesses to Me in Jerusalem, and in all Judea and Samaria,"* and then He told us WHERE to do it *"to the end of the earth,"* (ACTS 1:8).

"Too many Christians are stuffing themselves with gospel blessings while millions have never had a taste."
– Vance Havner

MAY 16

Jesus said, *"That which is born of the flesh is flesh, and that which is born of the Spirit is spirit,"* (JOHN 3:6). Spiritual life can only come from the Spirit! Your parents may have given you genes, but God gives you grace. Your parents look after your body, but God longs for your soul. You get your looks after your parents, but you get your longevity from your heavenly Father.

MAY 17

"If you're going through Hell, keep going." – Winston Churchill

MAY 18

If we take care of our character, God will take care of our reputation.

MAY 19

Those of little benefit to the Savior's cause are of little threat to Satan's cause.

MAY 20

When we open our Bible, God opens His mouth and speaks to us.

MAY 21

Greatness lies not in the possession of power, but rather in the right usage of that power.

MAY 22

You can tell a failure by the way he criticizes success. Those who can - DO! Those who can't – CRITICIZE!

MAY 23

As believers our convictions should be DOGMATIC. Our service should be AUTOMATIC. And our witness should be ENERGETIC.

MAY 24

"If sinners be damned, at least let them leap to Hell over our bodies. If they will perish, let them perish with our arms about their knees. Let no one go there unwarned and unprayed for." – Charles Spurgeon

MAY 25

"We must meet the uncertainties of this world with the certainty of the world to come." – A.W. Tozer

MAY 26

If you're dating someone who is selfish, you ain't seen nothing yet! Wait till you're married!

MAY 27

Without faults forgiveness would serve no purpose.

MAY 28

The one who takes lightly the guilt of sin will also take lightly the grace of forgiveness.

MAY 29

God's humbling of a man is not necessarily a reflection on a person's past as much as it is a requirement for a man's future.

MAY 30

Leadership is not giving up authority; it's giving away authority!

MAY 31

The important thing in life is not knowing all that God knows, but doing all that God says.

JUNE

JUNE 1

"Bad will be the day, for every man when he becomes absolutely contented with the life that he is living, with the thoughts that he is thinking, with the deeds that he is doing, when there is not forever beating at the doors of his soul some great desire to do something larger, which he knows that he was meant and made to do because he is still, in spite of all, the child of God." – Phillips Brooks

JUNE 2

Let us value positive action far above
pious appearance. The Pharisees
had a religious appearance, but their
actions proved they were far from
God. Good works are not the reason
of our salvation; they are the result of
our salvation.

◆ ◆ ◆

JUNE 3

If you don't believe in Satan, get
really serious about producing fruit for
the Kingdom of God and then you
will.

◆ ◆ ◆

JUNE 4

Slander only hurts the reputation
of a man, but seduction hurts the
character of a man.

JUNE 5

The practice of counseling and psychiatry void of biblical truth is like meeting a hungry man and giving him a toothpick.

JUNE 6

"Lord, when I am wrong, make me willing to change; when I am right, make me easy to live with. So strengthen me that the power of my example will far exceed the authority of my rank." – Pauline H. Peters

JUNE 7

Those who complain about the way the ball bounces are often the ones who dropped it.

JUNE 8

Blessed is the man who can hear his alarm clock as well on Sunday as he does on Monday!

JUNE 9

One of the basic lessons in the school of faith is: God's WILL must be fulfilled according to God's WAY and according to God's WATCH.

JUNE 10

Hell is a truth that is realized only too late.

JUNE 11

A broken home is like a broken nest; the eggs usually crack.

JUNE 12

Thankfully, the well of God's grace never runs dry.

JUNE 13

This date was my mother's birthday. Remembering her is easy, I do it everyday, but missing her is heartache that never goes away.

My mother lived 81 years and in all those years accumulated only one title – mom. Yet, other than the name of Jesus, it is the sweetest name I know.

JUNE 14

If God brought you to it, He will bring you through it.

JUNE 15

God gave children to parents, not to the school, not to the church, and not to the village. When it comes to rearing children, a father must often start at the rear.

Foolishness is bound up in the heart of a child; the rod of correction will drive it far from him (PROVERBS 22:15).

JUNE 16

A responsible father does not lower the standard of his home to accommodate the rebellion of his children.

JUNE 17

The father of the prodigal son teaches us that it is more important to be respected than to be liked. Father, you are a PARENT, not a PEER! God didn't give you children because they needed another buddy, but because they needed authority, direction, and leadership!

JUNE 18

The father of the prodigal son (LUKE 15:11-32) would make the Father's Hall of Fame, not because he had perfect children, but because he did not allow his children's WANTS and WISHES to determine the WAY he parented.

JUNE 19

A child's rebellion is not the result of superior wisdom or thinking, it is from hell! Our heavenly Father does not overlook rebellion; neither should earthly fathers.

JUNE 20

The prodigal son said, *"Father, GIVE ME the portion of goods that falls to me,"* (LUKE 15:12 emphasis mine). Rebellious children are more interested in acquiring than they are in allegiance.

JUNE 21

I praise my heavenly Father. He is my Abba, Father! My Daddy; my Papa. He provides for me; He protects me; He is patience with me; and He has pardoned me! He is gracious, merciful, long-suffering, and forgiving. He has adopted me, not because of who I am, but rather because of who He is. My inheritance as my Father's child will not be received in this world's currency, but rather in the riches of His kingdom!

I have very often disappointed my Father. He has never approved of my wrongdoing, nor has He lowered His standard to accommodate my wrongdoing. Yet, He always receives my confession and repentance, not with an accusing pointed finger, but rather with open arms of love and forgiveness. In the world I have learned the meaning of misery; in my Father's house I have learned the meaning of mercy.

I bless the name of my Father!

JUNE 22

Courage is not the absence of fear but rather the willingness to proceed in spite of it.

◆ ◆ ◆

JUNE 23

"Remember that the entire population of the universe, with one trifling exception, is composed of others." – J.A. Holmes

◆ ◆ ◆

JUNE 24

It's amazing how little time you have to feel sorry for yourself when you are busy changing the world! – Copied

JUNE 25

Why can't the government cut down on its spending? It's forced the rest of us to cut down on ours!

JUNE 26

It use to be that only Washington's face was on our money, but now Washington's hands on our money!

JUNE 27

I don't like to be pessimistic but I don't trust the government. There is too much overhead and too much underhand.

JUNE 28

The more government has to do with the economy, the less economy has to do with the government.

JUNE 29

Much has been said about what America stands for. I think it's time we bring back some of the things America wouldn't stand for!

JUNE 30

You cannot legislate the poor into prosperity, by legislating the wealthy out of prosperity. What one person receives without working for another person must work for without receiving. The government cannot give to anybody anything that the government does not first take from somebody else. You cannot multiply wealth by dividing it. When half of the people get the idea that they do not have to work because the other half is going to take care of them; and when the other half gets the idea that it does no good to work, because somebody else is going to get what they work for, that is the beginning of the end of any nation. – Copied

JULY

JULY 1

I think a believer should be more Christ-like than Baptist-like, Methodist-like, Presbyterian-like, etc. I think a citizen should be more American-like than Democrat-like, or Republican-like!

JULY 2

Nations die with the decreasing of convictions, which veils itself as the increasing of compassion.

JULY 3

The phrase "God bless America," is a popular one. We want God's blessing but do we really want God, and can we have His blessing and not have Him?

JULY 4

"Let the Fourth of July always be a reminder that here in this land, for the first time, it was decided that man is born with certain God-given rights; that government is only a convenience created and managed by the people, with no powers of its own except those voluntarily granted to it by the people." – Ronald Reagan

JULY 5

"This great nation was founded, not
by religionists, but by Christians, not
on religions but on the gospel of Jesus
Christ." – Patrick Henry

JULY 6

"I've lived, sir, a long time, and the
longer I live, the more convincing
proofs I see of this truth: That God
governs in the affairs of men. If a
sparrow cannot fall to the ground
without His notice, is it probable that
an empire can rise without His aid?
We've been assured in the sacred
writings that unless the Lord builds the
house, they labor in vain who build it.
I firmly believe this, and I also believe
that without His concurring aid, we
shall succeed in this political building
no better than the builders of Babel."
– Benjamin Franklin, signer of the
Declaration of Independence and
the Constitution

JULY 7

Freedom is not found in the JUDICIAL COURTS, but in JESUS CHRIST! *"If the Son makes you free, you shall be free indeed,"* (JN. 8:36).

◆ ◆ ◆

JULY 8

"No law can give me the right to do what is wrong." – Abraham Lincoln

◆ ◆ ◆

JULY 9

"Any society that would give up a little liberty to gain a little security will deserve neither and lose both." Benjamin Franklin

JULY 10

The Bible warns against debt. God said to Israel, *"you shall lend to many nations, but you shall not borrow; you shall reign over many nations, but they shall not reign over you."* (DEUT. 15:6). Strangely enough, it appears politicians are rewarded for spending money and punished for cutting back and stay within budget. It is almost as if our leaders are swiping our personal credit cards to get votes. The United States is know as the wealthiest country on earth, yet we borrow billions of dollars from other countries. It seems normal to me to think we should be the nation lending money and holding others in our debt, not the other way around.

JULY 11

Our government may make abortion LEGAL, but our government cannot make abortion MORAL! Quite frankly, I am appalled by the "preachers" that would trade in a biblical stance on abortion and same-sex marriage for a government run health care that would support both. Here is one ole hillbilly preacher that would trade in my health care to abolish abortion in a skinny minute! These preachers need to quit swimming with the cultural flow. Jesus' life would teach us that to be a follower of Christ would be counter-cultural! Jesus certainly wasn't crucified because He was in the flow and direction with the culture!

JULY 12

Laws reflect a nation's priorities, agenda, and values. When religion and God is separated from a society anything goes. When the law of man replaces the Law of Moses, society will drown in evil.

JULY 13

Either God is the lawgiver or man is. Either God is supreme or the sate is supreme!

JULY 14

When a government is accountable to no one except itself, it assumes that whatever is legal is moral.

PROVERBS 14:12 & 16:25 *There is a way that seems right to a man, but its end is the way of death.*

JULY 15

AS BELIEVERS...

Let us not trade in our Bible for bread.

Let us not trade in our conviction for convenience.

Let us keep our eyes on the Judge and not the judges.

Let us understand that the Supreme Court is not supreme.

Let us acknowledge that our hope is not on Pennsylvania Avenue, but on the streets of gold.

Let us value our heavenly citizenship over our earthly citizenship.

Let us trust in God, not in the government.

Let us live like Jesus says, and not as the state says.

JULY 16

Most of the Founding Fathers would not qualify or be approved, to serve in the Supreme Court today because of their religious convictions.

JULY 17

In a near future day, the Antichrist will use laws that will persecute those that do not worship him. *He shall speak pompous words against the Most High. Shall persecute the saints of the Most High. And shall intend to change times and law. Then the saints shall be given into his hand.* (emphasis mine DAN. 7:25). Like a master politician he will flatter and impress the people. He will promise the world that everyone will be better off with him in charge. He will deceive and dupe the people with his lies and falsehoods. He will then make laws, which allow him to control the economy and elevate himself to be the object of worship. The environment is being created today by a humanistic agenda that is on steroids.

JULY 18

"By clever and persevering use of propaganda even heaven can be represented as hell to the people."
– Adolf Hitler

JULY 19

We cannot depend on the media in America to tell us that truth any longer. They are far more concerned with their agenda, and in the end will betray the good of the nation for ratings!

JULY 20

Could I suggest that John the Baptist was executed for a "hate crime." This prophet of God told King Herod, *"It is not lawful for you to have your brother's wife." Therefore, Herodias held it against him and wanted to kill him,"* (MK. 6:18-19). To speak out against sin and evil is considered a "hate crime" by a secular society, and America is breaking the speed limit racing toward secularization. Will there be any of John the Baptist in us when all criticism of homosexuality is a hate crime? Will there be any prophet in us when all criticism of Islam, with its "honor killings" and Sharia law, is deemed a hate crime?

JULY 21

There are times when the government so abuses power as to command that we do something morally or spiritually wrong. There a believer must draw the line, even at the cost of imprisonment or death. We must not bow to the dictates of human authority in matters where it trespasses on divine authority.

JULY 22

A believer's greatest commitment is to a sovereign God, not a secular government; to the immutable One, not the ideological politician; and to the omniscience One, not the opportunistic one!

JULY 23

"Nothing is politically right that is
morally wrong." – Adrian Rogers

JULY 24

The propaganda among politicians
and the news media in America
today is just as bad, if not worse,
than was the propaganda machine
in Russia before the fall of the iron
curtain! Its intent is to camouflage
the citizenry of the truth in order to
promote one's own agenda!

JULY 25

Imagine a man whose wife is a spendthrift. He is a hard workingman who wants to provide for his family. Each year he brings home more and more income, but each year his wife spends more and more money. Several years down the road the wife has run household debt to an astronomical number. I ask you, does the problem lie with the husband who works hard and brings home more and more money, or does the problem lie with the wife who cannot operate within the household budget? The problem in this country is not with the citizens who love their country, work hard, and pay their taxes; the problem is with an out of control government who just keeps spending more and more and then wants you and I to believe the problem is that we are not taxed enough!

JULY 26

When the government is allowed to have more power, the more laws it will pass to diminish the role of the church!

JULY 27

"There is no worse tyranny than to force a man to pay for what he does not want, merely because you think it would be good for him."
– Robert A. Heinlein

JULY 28

"One of the great mistakes is to judge policies and programs by their intentions rather than their results."
– Milton Friedman

JULY 29

"Any society that would give up a little liberty to gain a little security will deserve neither and lose both."
– Benjamin Franklin

◆ ◆ ◆

JULY 30

It is wrong for politicians to use taxpayer's money to reward their supporters.

◆ ◆ ◆

JULY 31

"We the people are the rightful masters of both Congress and the Courts, not to overthrow the Constitution but to overthrow the men who would pervert the Constitution."
– Abraham Lincoln

AUGUST

AUGUST 1

Sinners do not have a weak defense in God's courtroom; they have no defense (PSA. 130:3).

AUGUST 2

"The only right a Christian has is the right to give up his rights."
– Oswald Chambers

AUGUST 3

Men look to find fame, but God looks to find faith.

AUGUST 4

The will to succeed is futile if not accompanied by the discipline of preparation and execution.

AUGUST 5

If it were not for the doers, the critics would soon be out of business.

AUGUST 6

The less bread of life a church has, the more casseroles, ice cream and cake it takes to keep it going.

AUGUST 7

God doesn't demand that we are RELIGIOUS; God demands that we are RIGHTEOUS!

AUGUST 8

"The bridge of grace will bear your weight, brother. Thousands of big sinners have gone across that bridge, yea, tens of thousands have gone over it. Some have been the chief of sinners and some have come at the very last of their days but the arch has never yielded beneath their weight. I will go with them trusting to the same support. It will bear me over as it has for them." – Charles Spurgeon

AUGUST 9

Sometimes God may lower our position and lessen our possessions so that He might strengthen our character.

AUGUST 10

Time is the greatest thing a leader will ever spend.

AUGUST 11

Giving back is difficult to do without first giving up.

AUGUST 12

"Your present circumstances don't determine where you go; they merely determine where you start."
– Nido Qubein

AUGUST 13

When God saves a person, He sends a person. Who among the redeemed has not been called of God to go? In our saving, God does not force us into salvation. In our sending, God does not force us into sharing. Like Isaiah, volunteer and say, *"Here am I! Send me"* (ISA. 6:9).

AUGUST 14

He who stays in the valley never makes it over the hill.

AUGUST 15

"Never argue with stupid people, they will drag you down to their level and then beat you with experience."
– Mark Twain

In the multitude of words sin is not lacking, but he who restrains his lips is wise. PROVERBS 10:19

AUGUST 16

LEADERSHIP is inspiration and
  motivation.
DICTATORSHIP is intimidation and
  manipulation.

AUGUST 17

When we disobey our heavenly
Father, He often takes us to the
woodshed. The Father's spankings
may hurt us but they never harm us.

AUGUST 18

A Pharisee is one who would torment themselves in this world only to gain nothing by it in the next. Phariseeism is the incarnation of legalism and they have many descendants in the church today.

AUGUST 19

A great and heavy burden is mine. As an unworthy, imperfect man embodied temporarily in human flesh, I have today the awesome responsibility and privilege to preach the perfect and eternal Word of God!

But we have this treasure in earthen vessels, that the excellence of the power may be of God and not of us (2 COR. 4:7).

111

AUGUST 20

Where there is an absence of grace, there will be an absence of relationships!

AUGUST 21

God's presence can make a prison a palace. On the other hand, God's absence can make a palace a prison.

AUGUST 22

The goal of a leader is not to build a bigger government, or a bigger business, or a bigger organization, or a bigger church, but rather a bigger people!

AUGUST 23

True leadership should bless the people, not benefit the leader.

AUGUST 24

"Every man must do two things alone: he must do his own believing and his own dying." – Martin Luther

AUGUST 25

For the believer, death lifts us above the SIGHTS of this world, the SOUNDS of this world, and the SIN of this world!

AUGUST 26

WHEREVER Christ is preached, and by WHOMEVER Christ is preached, it is Christ that saves!

AUGUST 27

Make a friend before you need a friend!

◆ ◆ ◆

AUGUST 28

"If you would not be forgotten as soon as you are dead, either write things worth reading or do things worth writing." Ben Franklin

◆ ◆ ◆

AUGUST 29

Leadership is not found in the hoarding of power, but rather in the handing out of power.

◆ ◆ ◆

AUGUST 30

The cave of lowliness often precedes the throne of loftiness (1 SAM. 22:1).

AUGUST 31

The great task of the church is
twofold: to get sinners into heaven
and saints out of bed!

SEPTEMBER

SEPTEMBER 1

The church today could use more calloused hands and a lot less of calloused hearts.

SEPTEMBER 2

You can tell what a man is made of by what he turns up when he is offered a job – his nose or his sleeves.

SEPTEMBER 3

The minimum wage continues to go up, now if we could just do something about minimum effort.

SEPTEMBER 4

Whether you hate your alarm clock,
or consider it a dear friend, says much
about your desire to achieve.

SEPTEMBER 5

Ambition is great but it never
accomplishes anything until it first
forms a partnership with work.

SEPTEMBER 6

Economists predict that the days
ahead will be prosperous for hard
workers. What a scary outlook for
many!

SEPTEMBER 7

You won't go far in life without enthusiasm, but neither will you go far in life if enthusiasm is all you have.

SEPTEMBER 8

Regarding Ishmael and his descendants, God said, *"He shall be a wild man; his hand shall be against every man, and every man's hand against him"* (GEN. 16:12).

From Ishmael the Arab tribes have descended to fulfill the role of destiny. They have found for themselves a prophet in Muhammad and have been forever the foe and enemy of Israel. The Arab people would trace their lineage back to Abraham and Ishmael; the Jews trace their lineage back to Abraham and Isaac. Today the Arabs sit on the oil reserves of the world and constantly threaten world peace. Their hatred for Israel keeps the world ever on the brink of war.

SEPTEMBER 9

Regarding Ishmael and his descendants, God said, *"He shall be a wild man; his hand shall be against every man, and every man's hand against him"* (GEN. 16:12).

In Islam you have a religion that is commissioned by Allah to rule the world. The idea is not that the whole world would become Muslim, but that the whole world would be subdued under the rule of Islam.

SEPTEMBER 10

Ishmael was Abraham's illegitimate son by the Egyptian maidservant Hagar. Ishmael would not be Abraham's heir in the blessings of the covenant. Abraham's other son was Isaac, given birth legitimately by his wife Sarah (GEN. 21:3). Regarding Isaac, God said that he was Abraham's *"only son"* (GEN. 22:2, 12, 16). The experience of Abraham and Isaac on Mount Moriah, gives to us a beautiful picture of Jesus' sacrifice for us on the cross.

SEPTEMBER 11

We all remember where we were
and what we were doing on
September 11, 2001.

Israel understands what the United
States has not yet understood: we
cannot have peace with Muslims
unless we submit to the rule of Islam,
or we are militarily stronger than they
are. Certainly there is the mentality
of jihad and open war with Muslim
countries and terrorists groups, but
thee is also war by infiltration, which
happened on September 11, 2001.
We better be paying attention to our
borders and immigration laws. There
are some 2,100 plus mosques within
the borders of the United States now.

Our government has a lackadaisical,
and even an unbiblical attitude,
regarding borders. Regarding Israel

they say you have no right to your borders. Regarding the Palestinians they say you have every right to your borders. To the citizens of the United States they say you have no borders.

SEPTEMBER 12

If what we care about is saving the lives of innocent human beings by reducing the number of mass public shootings and the deaths they cause, only one policy has ever been shown to work: concealed-carry laws. On the other hand, if what we care about is political grandstanding, and to brush aside the cold-blooded murder of innocent children, try the other policies.

SEPTEMBER 13

A man does not preach for the
INCOME, but for the OUTCOME!

SEPTEMBER 14

When grace is in your heart, your
hope is to release others from fear not
create it!

SEPTEMBER 15

Leadership can never be a one-man
show. When one insists on applause,
attention, and affirmation, he has no
room for others except to use them
for his benefit and ends up a one-
man show; and a one-man show is
not the stuff leaders are made of.

SEPTEMBER 16

Man's indifference to God soon degenerates into independence from God!

SEPTEMBER 17

We are not saved by making promises to God but by believing in the promises of God.

SEPTEMBER 18

"Backsliding begins when knee bending stops." – Unknown

SEPTEMBER 19

Difficult circumstances provide great opportunity for us to develop submissiveness, to behave humbly, and to react graciously.

SEPTEMBER 20

Upset us O Lord from the satisfaction of accomplished goals because we have dream too small.

SEPTEMBER 21

Church should to be a place where you can easily find God, and a place that makes it difficult for you to forget God.

SEPTEMBER 22

We are not to enlist people in the Lord's service to make them faithful; we enlist them in the Lord's service because they are faithful.

SEPTEMBER 23

The church's best gift to the world is grace; for it is the best gift the church has received itself. Yet, the world often views the church as DEVOID of grace rather than DISPENSERS of grace.

SEPTEMBER 24

A leader is one who has the SENSE to choose good men; the SELF-RESTRAINT to let them do the job; and the SECURITY to praise them for a job well done!

SEPTEMBER 25

The very moment you began to believe that you did something for your salvation is the very moment that you minimize and disregard the blood and work of Christ on the cross.

SEPTEMBER 26

"Service: doing something because it
matters. Self-serving: doing something
because it gets noticed."
– Allan Taylor

SEPTEMBER 27

The road to failure is curbed with
contentment, paved with satisfaction,
and striped with fear.

SEPTEMBER 28

"Never allow the thought, 'I am
no use where I am,' because you
certainly can be of no use where you
are not." – Oswald Chambers

SEPTEMBER 29

For a great cardiovascular workout, don't go to the gym; go to church! This workout will change your heart from, "Woe is me," to "Here am I! Send me," (ISA. 6).

SEPTEMBER 30

Much of our so-called worship today is but a demonstration of man-made religious activity and gyrations that fail to glorify the Lord.

OCTOBER

OCTOBER 1

It takes a shout of encouragement to overcome a whisper of criticism.

OCTOBER 2

Beware of the flesh it will sacrifice the future on the altar of the present.

OCTOBER 3

Some Christians have such a sour attitude you would think that they were baptized in persimmon juice.

OCTOBER 4

Hypocritical prayers have diarrhea of the mouth but constipation of the soul.

OCTOBER 5

The smallest of deeds is far greater than the largest of intentions. Be a blessing to someone today.

OCTOBER 6

Conceived in the heart of God and empowered by the Holy Spirit, the church was established by Jesus Himself who promised to build His church. Jesus never promised to build a parachurch ministry, a seminary, or a denomination. He did promise to build His church. Other organizations may do many worthy things, but that which is nearest to the Bridegroom is the Bride.

OCTOBER 7

The church has not been damaged by the PERSECUTION of the world, but rather by the POPULARITY with the world!

OCTOBER 8

"I consider that the chief dangers which confront the coming century will be religion without the Holy Ghost, Christianity without Christ, forgiveness without repentance, salvation without regeneration, politics without God, and heaven without hell."
– William Booth (1829-1912), founder of the Salvation Army

OCTOBER 9

Every leader will experience the sharp barbs of the critic. The way some people criticize you'd think they get paid for it. In a race the lead car never has a front-end accident. When you get kicked in the rear, you know you're out in front.

OCTOBER 10

A leader should replace the words **"Forward march!"** with the words, **"Follow me!"** Unless a leader is prepared to put himself up front and set the example, he does not qualify to command others.

OCTOBER 11

Good leaders are always stooping for it is the only way to reach down and pull others up.

OCTOBER 12

We are the Bibles the world is reading; we are the creeds the world is needing; we are the sermons the world is heeding. – Billy Graham

OCTOBER 13

All God needs to use you is all of you!

OCTOBER 14

There are thousands of ways to please God, but not one without faith! *"Without faith it is impossible to please God"* (HEB. 11:6).

OCTOBER 15

"It is not great talents God blesses so much as great likeness to Jesus." – Robert Murray M'Cheyne

OCTOBER 16

Some folks never answer God's call
because they're too busy trying to
figure out God's direction.

◆ ◆ ◆

OCTOBER 17

Two objects characterized Abraham
life: a tent and an altar. With a tent
we see Abraham's relationship
to this world; with an altar we see
Abraham's relationship to the world to
come.

OCTOBER 18

Joseph's brothers envied him (GEN. 37:11). Envy is the daughter of the devil, and her sister is named, not Alice, but Malice. Envy and malice usually work together. Envy causes inward pain when we see others succeed; malice produces inward satisfaction when we see others fail.

OCTOBER 19

In salvation God will get us out of the world, but until then He wants to get the world out of us.

OCTOBER 20

You can go to hell with church membership, but you cannot go to hell with Jesus!

OCTOBER 21

Drinking does not drown your problems...it only irrigates them.

◆ ◆ ◆

OCTOBER 22

If you can find a path with no obstacles, it probably doesn't lead anywhere. – Frank A Clark

◆ ◆ ◆

OCTOBER 23

When you are promoted up in life your friends know you; when you fall down in life you know your friends.

◆ ◆ ◆

OCTOBER 24

Wise decisions are the result of an inner voice, not an outward look.

OCTOBER 25

"There are no office hours for champions." – Paul Dietzel

OCTOBER 26

Without God, a week would be: Sinday, Mournday, Tearsday, Wasteday, Thirstday, Fightday, and Shatterday. – Copied

OCTOBER 27

Regarding doing God's will, delay is the road that leads to defeat.

OCTOBER 28

Knowing God's Word and God's will, allows you to be aware of the circumstances that oppose God's Word and God's will.

OCTOBER 29

We are continually faced with opportunities that are brilliantly disguised as insoluble problems.

OCTOBER 30

God's calling: Loving what God has given you to do more than success, fame, or money.

OCTOBER 31

When the past calls, let it go to voicemail. It has nothing new to say.
– Copied

NOVEMBER

NOVEMBER 1

I think a believer should not vote PARTY but PRINCIPLE. Don't let the word of a politician make up your mind, let the Word of God make up your mind.

NOVEMBER 2

The problem in Washington, D.C., is that it is filled with those who have a career, but not a calling. When you have a career, your focus is on yourself and advancing your own ambitions. When you have a calling, your focus is on purpose and others. What we have is master politicians; what we don't have is servant leaders!

NOVEMBER 3

The citizens of this country are over-taxed, over-burdened, over-charged, over-run, overwhelmed, and under-led.

NOVEMBER 4

What this country needs is a leader who delivers more than they promise, not a politician who promises more than they can deliver.

NOVEMBER 5

We know Christ is coming, but so is the Antichrist!

As governments grow larger, the rights of the people grow smaller, and taxation grows larger. This paves the way for the world rule of the Antichrist and a one-world government.

As the conditions of economic systems become more interactive worldwide, it paves the way for the Antichrist, the mark of the beast, and a one-world economy.

As God and His Word continue to be removed from society and the human conscious, it leaves a void of soul and paves the way for the Antichrist to be worship in a one-world religion.

NOVEMBER 6

Congress has passed a gazillion laws yet cannot improve on the Ten Commandments that they want to legislate out of our view.

NOVEMBER 7

There was a day when America was less dependent on the government and more dependent on God; today we are less dependent on God and more dependent on the government. Do you think we are better off?

NOVEMBER 8

"A vote is like a rifle: its usefulness depends upon the character of the user." – Theodore Roosevelt

NOVEMBER 9

The cost of government will never GO DOWN unless the voters RISE UP!

NOVEMBER 10

Thousands of years ago God
gave to us through Moses the
Ten Commandments. Since then
the United States Supreme Court
has handed down the eleventh
commandment, "Thou shalt not, in
any classroom, read the first ten."

NOVEMBER 11

I AM...

A believer in Christ before I am
a Baptist (or Methodist, or
Presbyterian, or _____).

A citizen of heaven before I am a
citizen of the U.S.A.

A follower of Christ before I am a fan
of the Tennessee Volunteers (or any
other team).

Devoted to the truths of the Bible
before I am a Democrat or
Republican!

NOVEMBER 12

If alcoholism is a disease...
It is the only one to be bottled and
 sold.
It is the only one that requires a
 license to propagate it.
It is the only one that requires outlets
 to spread it.
It is the only one that produces
 revenue for the government.
It is the only disease without a germ or
 virus.
Um, maybe it's not a disease after all?

NOVEMBER 13

Indecision, in the end is a decision
after all.

NOVEMBER 14

Our response to adversity will determine whether our troubles will curse us or bless us.

NOVEMBER 15

Procrastinated responsibility is like an unpaid bill; it is only deferred, and will eventually return demanding the account be settled and with interest.

NOVEMBER 16

A humble man never blows his "knows" in public.

NOVEMBER 17

Limited success is the result of limited obedience.

NOVEMBER 18

The differences between worry and concern: worry sees a problem concern solves the problem.

NOVEMBER 19

You may know ten thousand other things, but that will never suffice for the failure to know the will of God.

NOVEMBER 20

The Bible's goal is not for the deformed to be informed, but for the deformed to be transformed!

NOVEMBER 21

If you can live up to the message you preach, it is very possible you are not preaching much of a message.

NOVEMBER 22

With the socialistic leanings of our government leaders today, I wonder what President John F. Kennedy, who was assassinated on this day in 1963 would say. Here is what he did say, "My fellow Americans, ask not what your country can do for you, ask what you can do for your country."

NOVEMBER 23

Today is my birthday, and how do I feel about that? I love birthdays but too many of them will kill a feller.

NOVEMBER 24

Where there is an absence of teamwork, there will be an absence of victories!

NOVEMBER 25

Jesus said, *"Beware of false prophets, who come to you in sheep's clothing, but inwardly they are ravenous wolves."* (MATT. 7:15).

A false prophet never INTENDS to be what he PRETENDS to be.

NOVEMBER 26

"The nose of the bulldog is slanted backwards so he can continue to breathe without letting go."
– Winston Churchill

Never give up in the dark what God gave you in His light.

NOVEMBER 27

"By perseverance the snail reached the ark." – Charles Spurgeon

Interest alone never gets the job done. It takes commitment, persistence, and endurance!

NOVEMBER 28

God's gift to you is not a loan; it's a deposit but it needs your interest.

NOVEMBER 29

Walking backward can never take you into the future. Don't allow your past mistakes to become memorials. They should be cremated, not embalmed.

...forgetting those things which are

behind and reaching forward to those things which are ahead, I press toward the goal for the prize of the upward call of God in Christ Jesus (PHIL. 3:13-14).

NOVEMBER 30

An army of sheep led by a lion would defeat an army of lions led by a sheep.

...the Lord spoke to Joshua...arise, go over this Jordan...every place that the sole of your foot will tread upon I have given you...be strong and very courageous... (JOSH. 1:1-3, 7).

DECEMBER

DECEMBER 1

There are three objects that are emblematic of Jesus: a cradle, a cross, and a crown. The focus of the Christmas season is the cradle.

Christ's cradle was promised. Some 700 years before His birth Jesus' birth was promised. *"Therefore the Lord Himself will give you a sign: Behold, the virgin shall conceive and bear a Son, and shall call His name Immanuel"* (ISA. 7:14). Isaiah's reports that His name would be Immanuel, yet nowhere in the Gospels was Christ ever called Immanuel which means God with us. He was called Jesus because He would save people from

their sins (MATT. 1:21), but He cannot
save people from their sins unless He is
Immanuel, God with us.

DECEMBER 2

Christ's cradle was pure. Now the birth
of Jesus Christ was as follow: *After
His mother Mary was betrothed to
Joseph, before they came together,
she was found with child of the Holy
Spirit* (MATT. 1:18).

The purity of Jesus' birth is absolutely
necessary if indeed He is the one
to die and make atonement for
my sin. You and I cannot die for
the atonement of our own sin, let
alone the sin of the world for we are
unacceptable for we are sinners,
conceived and born into sin. How can
Jesus be our Savior? Because He is
Immanuel, God with us. And how did

He get to be with us? He was born of a
virgin and conceived by the Holy Spirit.

DECEMBER 3

Christ's cradle was planned. The first
coming of Christ was announced
in the Garden as God spoke to
the serpent, *"And I will put enmity
between you and the woman, and
between your seed and her Seed; He
shall bruise your head, and you shall
bruise His hell"* (GEN. 3:15).

God mentions Eve's offspring, not
Adam's offspring. The Adamic nature
is one of sin. Every man who has had
an earthly father was and is a sinner.
Back in the Garden God proclaimed
that there is One who is coming who
will be of Eve but not Adam. Here
in the beginning days of time, God
announces the virgin birth of Christ.

155

DECEMBER 4

The message of the world's religions is that mankind is in search of God, but the message of Christianity is that God is in search of mankind. After Adam and Eve sinned, God searched for them and called to Adam saying, *"Where are you?"* (GEN. 3:9). Now at the first Christmas here comes Jesus who comes for the expressed purpose *"to seek and to save that which was lost"* (LK. 19:10). Jesus is *the Lamb slain from the foundation of the world* (REV. 13:8).

Salvation was in the heart of God long before sin was in the heart of man.

DECEMBER 5

As the pregnant Mary traveled the road from Nazareth to Bethlehem she was full of Jesus. As we travel the road from this earth to Heaven, may we be full of Jesus.

DECEMBER 6

Jesus was born in a stable so that you and I could be born again to live in a mansion!

DECEMBER 7

At the birth of Jesus, Herod was exceedingly angry; and he sent forth and put to death all the male children who were in Bethlehem...from two years old and under (MATT. 2:16). All this insecure king could think of was death, and at the time One had come to conquer it.

DECEMBER 8

The wise men had come and asked Herod, *"Where is He who has been born King of the Jews?"* (MATT. 2:2). The thought of another king sent jealous and insecure Herod into a frenzy of fear and anger. He ordered the slaughter of all the infant male children in his effort to snuff out any threat to his throne. It reminds me of our politicians today who will not make a stand against the horror of abortion. Like Herod, making a stand regarding abortion will cost them reelection; it will cost them their throne. Many will not allow Jesus to sit on the throne of their life for fear that they may have to dismount that throne first.

The wise men were delighted with Jesus; Herod was disturbed with Jesus. Does Jesus delight you or disturb you?

DECEMBER 9

Upon hearing of Jesus' birth, Herod *gathered all the chief priests and scribes of the people together* (MATT. 2:4). These priests and scribes knew the facts of Old Testament prophecies concerning the Messiah's birth, but showed no concern for Jesus' birth. Their problem wasn't the facts; their problem was faith. They told King Herod facts of scripture but showed no interest in the birth of Jesus. They were within five to six miles of the birth of God's Son, but were completely apathetic and indifferent. Like these religious leaders you can be so close to Jesus, yet be so satisfied with yourself and your own self-righteousness, that you have no desire to see Jesus.

DECEMBER 10

The wise men *rejoiced with exceedingly great joy* when they saw the star that would lead them to Jesus (MATT. 2:10). They had a strong desire to find Jesus. If you are sincerely trying to find Jesus, you will succeed. The same grace that led the wise men to find Jesus is available to you today. The Bible is clear to point out that the wise men worshiped Jesus. They *fell down and worshiped Him* (MATT. 2:11). The wise men were delighted to meet both Mary and Joseph, but it was Jesus that they sought and Jesus that they worshiped.

O come, let us adore Him, Christ the Lord!

DECEMBER 11

Christmas is all about giving and receiving. God gave His Son and we must receive Him. There are three things that must be present to receive a gift: There has to be a GIFT. The Bible tells us *"the gift of God is eternal life"* (ROM. 6:23).

There has to be a GIVER. To receive a gift someone must offer you a gift. *"For God so loved the world that He gave His only begotten Son,"* (JN. 3:16). There has to be GRACE. Since it is impossible to earn, or merit a gift, the giver gives on the basis of grace. *"For by grace you have been saved,"* (EPH. 2:8). Salvation is not a reward, it is a free gift based on the grace of God.

DECEMBER 12

Jesus was *the glory as of the only begotten of the Father, full of grace and truth* (JN. 1:14). Grace would be the overflow of God's LOVE. Truth would be the substance of God's LAW. In Christ, both were in perfect balance.

DECEMBER 13

And the Word became flesh and dwelt among us (JN. 1:14). He pitched His tent, and tabernacle here among us. This thought takes us back some 1,400 years to Moses. God told Moses He had decided to come down to earth and live with His people. What grace! He came from the mansions of glory, and from the brilliancy of His throne, surrounded by countless angels who hung upon His every word and rushed to do His will. Yet down to earth He came to dwell in the midst of His pilgrim people. Isn't that just like Him?

DECEMBER 14

John informs us: *In the beginning was the Word* (JN. 1:1). This does not refer to a start but a state. Jesus is the second Person of the Godhead, yet *the Word became flesh* (JN. 1:14). He assumed humanity and inhabited a body of flesh and blood. John further explains, *and the Word was with God* (JN. 1:1): a separate Person within the Godhead. That He became flesh means that God became a Man. There now lives a Man who is God.

DECEMBER 15

LUKE 2:7 *And she brought forth her firstborn Son, and wrapped Him in swaddling cloths, and laid Him in a manger, because there was no room for them in the inn.*

There was no room for them in the inn. Perhaps Joseph pleaded his case. "Look here Mr. Innkeeper, do you have any idea who we are? My wife and me are descendants of King David. The Child to be born is the rightful heir to David's throne. You can't allow Him to be born on the street." The innkeeper said, "Alright then, use the cattle shed."

Thus it was that the Lord of glory arrived on planet Earth by way of a virgin's womb, born in a barn, and laid in a manger. The Creator of the universe was born of all places, in a barn with manure for carpeting and cobwebs for curtains. While men slept and angels sang, and the innkeeper retired to his room and to his bed, a miracle of miracles took place that night in His barn. The Son of God became the Son of Man so that the sons of men might become the sons of God.

DECEMBER 16

ISAIAH 9:6 *For unto us a Child is born, unto us a Son is given; and the government will be upon His shoulder. And His name will be called Wonderful, Counselor, Mighty God, Everlasting Father, Prince of Peace. [7]Of the increase of His government and peace there will be no end…*

- Isaiah says, a Child is born…a Son is given.
- Matthew and Luke tell us of the

Child that was born.

John tells of the Son that was given.

- The Child born – points us to the Son of man.

The Son given – points us to the Son of God.

- The Child born was the Babe of Bethlehem.

The Son given was the Lord from heaven.

- The Child born reminds us that He was a Man.

The Son given reminds us that He was God.

- The Child born marks the beginning of time.

The Son given is the ancient of days, from everlasting to everlasting.

Jesus was both the Child born, and the Son given.

DECEMBER 17

Jesus did not come from Heaven to earth to offer us something we could refuse and still be all right!

DECEMBER 18

God has a CURSE for sin; He sent Adam out of the garden (GEN. 3:23). God has a CURE for sinners; you shall call His name Jesus, for He will save His people from their sins (MATT. 1:21).

DECEMBER 19

The greatest of all gifts comes not in a SLEIGH, but in a STABLE.

DECEMBER 20

On that first Christmas, the quiet and humble carpenter, Joseph, stepped up and became the adoptive father of Jesus. Twelve years later he would step down, realizing Jesus' first allegiance must be to another Father (Lk. 2:49).

DECEMBER 21

What's in a name? After all isn't a name just a collection of alphabet letters? And whose idea was it on that first Christmas to call the Child Jesus? Well it was God's idea, like any father, He wanted to name His own Son. An angel of the Lord told Joseph, *"You shall call His name Jesus, for He will save His people from their sins"* (MATT. 1:21). Jesus is the Greek equivalent of Joshua, and it means "God saves." God the Father chose a name for His Son with past significance. Joshua was the one who led Israel into their Promised Land. After centuries of slavery and bondage, and forty years of wilderness wandering, Joshua would cross a barrier that had seemed insurmountable – the Jordan River. When Jesus was some thirty years old, He would be baptized in that same river. He would later die, be buried, and then resurrect from the grave, crossing a barrier that was insurmountable for mankind. Now after years of slavery to sin and wandering on this earth, He leads us to the Promised Land of heaven. What's in a name? *"There is no other name under heaven given among men by which we must be saved"* (ACTS 4:12) for *God also has highly exalted Him and given Him the name which is above every name* (PHIL. 2:9).

DECEMBER 22

The first visitors to the nativity were shepherds: common men, uneducated men, and unsophisticated men. God, it seems, is always confounding our notions of how life is suppose to be. After all, Jesus would say, *"whoever desires to become great among you, let him by your servant"* (MATT. 20:26). He would choose unlikely Bethlehem as the birthplace rather than Rome, or Athens, or even Jerusalem. He would choose Israel, a downtrodden occupied country, and for earthly parents He would choose peasants. On the night of Jesus' birth who received invitations to greet the newborn king? Was it the world's emperors and rulers? Was it the priests and prophets? Was it soldiers or scholars? No, it was shepherds. Whatever their names, they were found on the guest list of this newborn king. In David, Israel's second king, God made a shepherd into a king; in Jesus, Israel's last king, God made a king into a sacrificial lamb.

DECEMBER 23

As a king incognito, Jesus was born to a peasant couple and in an animal stable, certainly not the typical birth of a king, but God's ways run counter to man's ways. He came to turn the world and its values upside down. He came to show us that true greatness would be found in serving, not ruling. Jesus would say, *"Blessed are the meek"* (MATT. 5:5). Could such a message be received when delivered from a palace balcony? How many worldly kings have ever embrace lepers or mingled with society's most rejected people...but Jesus did.

DECEMBER 24

Throughout the Old Testament, God had sent His prophets many times, but now He would do something far more startling. He would vacate His throne in heaven, for a manger in an animal stall: a king in disguise, the Lord of the universe, the Creator among His creatures.

And the Word became flesh and dwelt among us, and we beheld His glory, the glory as of the only begotten of the Father... (JN. 1:14).

DECEMBER 25

Happy birthday to Jesus, the Creator, the ageless One, the ancient of days, the Alpha and Omega, the beginning and the end, from everlasting to everlasting. Happy birthday to the King of Glory, the King of kings and the Lord of lords, the prince of peace, the wonderful Counselor, mighty God and the lover of my soul. Happy birthday to Jesus: the Son of God, and the Son of man. The Lamb who bled and died for my salvation, the Lion who will defeat Satan and all his forces, and my Bridegroom who will greet me at the marriage supper and be forever mine! WELL GLORY!

DECEMBER 26

In the first moments after birth, new parents gaze in the face of their child. Can you imagine how intently Joseph and Mary must have studied the Child who came to them in Bethlehem? In the starlight they looked into the face of Him who is the light of the world.

DECEMBER 27

The Child that toddled behind Mary in His infancy is the Man that Mary followed behind in His adulthood: all the way to the cross, to the tomb, and to eternity.

DECEMBER 28

Having an earthly mother, Jesus was the Son of Man. Having a heavenly Father, Jesus was the Son of God. He was fully human and fully divine, simultaneously. Nothing about His humanity could detract from His deity; nothing about His deity could detract from His humanity. A Man of both worlds, only He can reconcile the Father in heaven with the people of the earth. Jesus is the bridge by which God comes to earth, and the bridge by which mankind comes to heaven! Because He is all man and all God, He is our all in all!

DECEMBER 29

How could we ever follow His footsteps as a man, had we not seen Him crawl as a child?

DECEMBER 30

An obscure son of a carpenter, from a no nothing town, in an occupied country, changed the world.... and after His death!

DECEMBER 31

Jesus' homeless birth in an animal stable prefigured His homeless life. Jesus said, *"Foxes have holes and birds of the air have nests, but the Son of Man has nowhere to lay His head"* (MATT. 8:20). The homelessness of Jesus has provided for us a mansion in heaven!